BLOofer

CW00351578

Dr Cathleen Allyn Conway (she/her) is a journalist, scholar, and academic. She earned her PhD in creative writing (poetry) from Goldsmiths, University of London. She is the author of *Nocturnes* (Cherry Dress Press, 2023), *American Ingénue* (Broken Sleep Books, 2021), *All the Twists of the Tongue* (Grey Book Press, 2018), and *Static Cling* (Dancing Girl Press, 2012). Originally from Chicago, she lives in London. @CatAllynC.

Also by Cathleen Allyn Conway

Nocturnes	(Cherry Dress Chapbooks, 2023)
American Ingénue	(Broken Sleep Books, 2021)
All the Twists of the Tongue	(Grey Book Press, 2018)
Static Cling	(Dancing Girl Press, 2012)

ISBN: 978-1-915760-10-4

The author has asserted their right to be identified as the author of this Work in accordance with the Copyright, Designs and Patents Act 1988

Cover designed by Aaron Kent

Edited & Typeset by Aaron Kent

Broken Sleep Books Ltd
Rhydwen
Talgarreg
Ceredigion
SA44 4HB

Broken Sleep Books Ltd
Fair View
St Georges Road
Cornwall
PL26 7YH

Contents

Bloofer

Cathleen Allyn Conway

She is the vampire of us all. So she supports us,
Fattens us, is kind. Her mouth is red.
I know her. I know her intimately—
Old winter-face, old barren one, old time bomb.
Men have used her meanly. She will eat them.

— SYLVIA PLATH
Three Women: A Poem for Three Voices, 1962

When other little girls wanted to be ballet dancers,
I kind of wanted to be a vampire.

— ANGELINA JOLIE

During the past two or three days several cases have occurred of young children straying from home or neglecting to return from their playing on the Heath. In all these cases the children were too young to give any properly intelligible account of themselves, but the consensus of their excuses is that they had been with a 'bloofer lady.' It has always been late in the evening when they have been missed, and on two occasions the children have not been found until early in the following morning.

— BRAM STOKER
Dracula, 1897

Urbane Gothic

Impossible city, preposterous city.
I smell them before I see them.

All powders, perfumes and oils
the half-smart creepy girls smear on.

There it is, underneath the sweet
subtle tang old skool goth,

the impossibly high cheekbones:
Fashion junkies. Pale creepy girls

who don't like sunlight and can't be
seen. Unclean. Unclean.

Thoughts bump against each other, afraid
the silence will reach out and grab them.

In the long run they're already dead.
Reflections like thoughts floating on glass,

as if melting into the underwater lights
of Times Square, thick and swirly, blinking

a sordid invitation outside the window.
But the city. Creepy girls are everything.

The Silence Inside Her

Don't touch me. I'm unclean. Jesus.
Give me my bag. I've waited too long.
Tears like vinegar. She bit me.

Wrap the dirty filthy blood-pressure
mouth-cuff and pump my lean, unripen heart.
I can't believe I waited so long.

I actually had an erection. Well, I'm not
most girls. I'm not even a girl, technically.
Put the stethoscope on my chest; listen.

If I'm dirty from her, it'll... do something to me.
Reading is 00/00. I do not tell you the nightmare.
Her lips on me... biting me... I liked it.

If you hadn't been here, I would have let her.
Dope. Great invention.
This is what PMS used to feel like.

Can you bandage my neck? Okay.
Tell me quick, darling, tell me now.
There's one more thing I have to do.

My sleight-of-hand is wearing out. See
the hammer glimmer in the flashlight glow?
Here. Look at me a minute.

The Villagers Never Liked You

I wake to a mausoleum.
This is the room I could never breathe in.

Black bat airs wrap me, raggy shawls,
blue garments unloosing small owls.

Eternity bores me; my soul dies for it.
I eat men like air. I never wanted it.

The Rising

The town knows about darkness, the slithered purple
that comes on the land when rotation hides the sun.
Something gathered, slow and heavy and electric, almost
as though the town knows evil is coming, and its shape.

From here we can't see spots on the sun. We know
where the roads go and where, how the ground lies.
The town has us because we know it, and it knows us.
It sees through our lies, even the ones we tell ourselves.

And in the dark, the town is ours and we are the town's.
Being in the town is prosaic, sensuous, alcoholic;
black galaxies shot with morphic red. We see ourselves
drowning in the sweet evil falls and liking it.

There is no life here but the slow death of days.
Something is going to happen. Can't we feel it?

Nothing

If I turned out to not be a girl,
would you still like me?
I'm not a boy. I'm nothing.
Not a child. Not old. Not a girl.
I'm just me. Is that disgusting?

I have always been intrigued by journals.
They are like dollhouses: you look
inside them and see a preserved self.
Every door is my door, just for me.

If I turned a girl, would you still like me?
If I turned a girl like me? What do you think I am?
I can be the princess, so cold and so fair.
What if I turned out to be the dragon?

The whole world is too small and I
am trapped inside it. Everyone is boxes
inside boxes for girls not ready to face
the big mean world of men and sex.

Please, you must neither move nor speak.
I hate promises. Promise me.
Just lie there on the stones.
Promise me and forgive me.

His Name Is Outside My Door

Love cannot come here. It was not love.
or missing him.
Or attached
to any emotion I could recognise.
I am fixed in this parenthesis.

I remember the minute I knew for sure:
love welled in my heart with a slow pain.
The soul curdles, still it seeps up, unexhausted.
The curse burns inside and makes you an unclean
thing, heat and tingle around your wounds.
Your body starts to decay faster than it should.

I sip instant coffee, grey and diffuse as weather.
He exhales and lies fill the air. He dreams in lies.

Pretend You Are Drowning

I couldn't understand why Marco was so hot.
I thought perhaps it was because he came from Peru

that everything about him felt so fiery and so dry.
His hands burned, and his mouth burned,

and his words burned until I burned.
My first wounded thought was for my dress.

A dark, damp shape worked out a loose, bulky bundle.
Marco knelt in the dark; descending, descending:

Then I untied the belt of my dressing gown.
In that light, the blood looked black.

Lagoon

Something happens in there. Something magical,
something evil.

They come at night. They gather around my bed,
they take me to a room

with this green light and a chair
with straps, as if for a surgeon.

Sunlight burns my skin like raging candlewax—
sunlight: portable ultraviolet fire.

Then ten thousand husbands wait in the water.
Then they fill me with their blood.

Dissertation

They're giving a lecture on basilisks tonight.
We always get round to De Quincey,
although we were supposed to be studying Poetics,
the marmoreal coldness of Blake's death mask,
and I. A. Richards in his early lecturing days.

Poems written out loud, about four in the morning,
before the glassy music of the milkman,
settling his bottles. It is December. It is foggy.
The two strains marry and paralyze each other.
Antique rosemary sprigs in orange punch.

This little woodcut of the Inquisition is so beautiful.

We Were in Paris

You had a branding iron
and there were worms in my baguette.
My tummy was growly. And you were out.
I want a treat. I need a treat.
You've been a very bad daddy.

My mother ate lemons. Raw.
She loved the way they made her mouth tingle.
Her favourite was custard. Brandied pears. Pomegranates.
They used to make her face and fingers all red.
Remember little fingers? Little hands? Do you?
Shhhhhh. Bite your tongue.
They used to eat. Cake. Eggs. Honey.
Until you came and ripped their throats out.

You remember that kind of hungry?
Don't worry. I'll see that you get strong again.
Like me.

The Girl He Met in the Park

In the fall, night comes like this hammer:
The sun loses its thin grip on the air, the cellar
fills with hot, coppery odor, turning cold.

She writhes on the table. Her hands beat
madly at the air like birds. Winter is coming.
His brain whirls with unremembered images.

Winter will be long. Her mouth yawns, revealing
shadows. There are no trees leaves to thicken;
faint light only a suggestion of something cheated.

Gaunt shadows bite the mean ground like teeth.

Her Sweet Purity

I could see in the white flesh: a dint.
Then I struck with all my might:
contorting and cut, The Thing writhed,
a blood-curdling screech from red lips.

I never faltered, deeper driving
my stake in the body, twisting and wild,
crimson foam smearing white,
blood from the pierce welling, welling.

The teeth ceased to champ,
the writhing became less.
On my forehead sprang
drops of sweat, broken gasps
came my breath, and a light broke
The Thing's face, glad and strange.

A Moment's Courage and Then It Is Done

Strike the blow that sets her free.
A blessed hand.
A blessed hand shall strike the blow.

Arthur saw what we all did –
that his should be the hand:
his hand that sent her to the stars;
his hand that loved her best;
the hand she herself would have chosen.

There lay Lucy, trembling.
Van Helsing said to him,
'And now you may kiss her.'

He stepped forward,
struck the blow that
restored Lucy as holy.

Arthur bent and kissed her.
She is not a grinning devil now.

Sangfroid

We're all drawn to what we're afraid of:

Pumping hearts heated the air like Paris, where I drank
the champagne of a mezzo-soprano at her salon in Montparnasse.
I was infatuated; I am still. I couldn't stand being a passing fancy.

Her face felt hot, her tongue a distant throbbing lit from inside,
bodies pressed so close the swell of her breasts were knobbed quartz,
the cant of her hips a window left open to the night.

I gripped her arms as she pushed my back into the dirt, wrestling
next to the *poubelles*, my breath catching in surprise under the soft
pressure of a mouth gliding over tiny hairs standing along my thigh.

Holding me in place, laving my skin, her tongue deep in my
garnets, red walls wincing with every hitch in my breath,
her hand a shiver like some slow electric current.

She didn't want to explain the recklessness, the pain of deep dream sleep.
Reeling back, I wake restless from red-soaked dreams,
worn down from a fear so deep it lives in my bones.

Close:

Being transformed.
Becoming white yet robust,
bright-eyed but crazed.
She shakes her beautiful curls
and dust falls from them.
She takes out scissors, cuts her hair.
She stands before the dressing table,
holding her long hair with both hands,
screaming and screaming.

Letter from Vampire Haven

I had fallen
into a new way of being vampire.
How unsure I was of my vampire a year ago.
If I want to keep on being a triple-threat vampire
I can't be a drudge,
but even now I vampire to myself.

Whether or not I am any vampire,
I will keep vamping,
purely from necessity.

Perhaps you will be vampiric,
even if I vamp at too much length.
Gradually I will evolve to other vampires.

I just want you to understand that vampires are responsible.

Career Girl

He appears unhoped for,
uncalled for, following her

inside,
closing the door.

He looks at her
with undisguised desire.

She looks at her file folder, her
hands, the books, the machine.

She feeds documents. The machine
rises and falls of its own accord.

He takes up space
that doesn't belong to him.

He picks up the finished copies, offers
hypnotic promises.

She quickly collates.
He sees the flesh and knows the future.

Death is where he's going.
She holds the door open.

Letter from ▇▇▇▇

I left you the face of S—, a green eye, a tooth:
small tokens that death has not put its blush on.
Her lips glow appetite-deep for the first time.
Pictures of this face still float loose in our city.

Fear of sounds, not of night, almost saved her life:
insidious whispers, soft laughter. Then sharp-fingered,
grabbing hands, hungry mouths, and in the end,
only the spiraling, exquisite pain swirls. On little girls,

the smooth fold of skin is no different than an eyelid.
The cells on my fingertips rubbed off and are still there.
I left her for you, wrapped in silence, to warm the place
where I occupied days, cold corpse beneath stone.

Red lips, yellow teeth, blood down her throat.
Be congenial. I have no further need of her.
Will her eyes open, red swirls, as you pump
into her cold body? Will her mouth? So.

Let us see how you like those girls, some not thirteen,
all colours and impressions and perfumes,
corruption their only knowledge of the world,
wonder-swallowed words come too soon.

Her Name

was a charm to ward off spirits.
She's an obsession: pure and sweet and chaste,
the sort to follow doom around with a guidebook.

She killed everyone she loved, stared into that golden
furnace, thinking her mad virgin flesh wouldn't burn.
She fled to a convent, and I sent back the key:

I gave her a demon when she took her orders.
I'm always trying to pry them apart,
like children caught in angry mobs.

Their names became one word that don't belong together.
Sometimes the truth is worse. The worst is to come,
if only for the few seconds her name is on my tongue.

The Three

He proposes like
a Magic 8 ball.
That makes two
proposals in one
day. I'm hoping
for three; longer
boats mixed up
with keys and
doors and distant
shores. I'm as
happy as a
wild storm between
my legs. He's
so fresh, like
something not quite
dead, like driftwood
rising and falling
on ocean swells.
There's enough of
me to share;
even dusk is
my escort. Why
can't a girl
marry as many
as want her?

I'll float away;
lose them. They're
little boys, flowing
over me like
a wave breaking
over my head
and I am
lost under water,
unsure if I'll
ever surface, not
caring if I
do. He has
an immense asylum
under his care,
a locked castle;
dormer windows and
sloped roofs and
tall red chimneys
and copper ornaments.
I'm afraid shelter
feels like a tomb.
He would just
do for you.

At Least I'm Pretty

Her eyebrows mock me in the mirror.   She sways;
                    limbs so smooth, so willowy-tall.
                    Brackish liquid dribbles

down her legs. Her luminous lips move.
I can't find my face in that silver veil.

Maybe   a vampire takes over someone else
            not to see their reflection in a mirror,
            but in another person's face. Her face

ethereal, her feathery voice a seasick wall of sound.
The faces of virgins aren't even pretty.

I'll never be like this,   hair rising in jeopardy flames, a pearl-fluid
            breeze in a clock-cry of stillness, a
            demon of doom tilting on a trapeze.

My brain will never work right.
I need to study the dark until it takes shape.

18 and Still Human

Look at her. Who is she; it doesn't say?
She's pretty coiffed:

unravelled red roses singing in her hair, drinking her coffee
like original sin, wounding with a flourish of her fatal whip.

It'll hurt like hell.

In Bluebeard's study he makes love to her cold dissected body
on a narrow cot, doing it every night whether her heart wants
it or not, every time like the first time.

Imagine:

enter her realm, become part of it, the light and shrieks and
mysterious symbols and language left by clarion birdmarks in
sand, phantoms that swim from the recesses of memory,

thin little girls with shadowed eyes and bloody thighs.

Imagine: 18 and still

Her Twilight World

Look, I know you feel like shit and you should feel like shit.

You are going to get well, I know it.

Your blood is a personal, intimate thing.

You're good and kind; you care about people.

No wonder everyone loves you.

I hate you so fucking much.

Remember the time I tried to take that boy away from you?

I would have killed someone for doing that to me.

I'd never even kissed a boy before.

Meeting him is the only good thing to happen to me.

But you were always the one, sinking deeper and deeper into twilight language.

I'd have been happy to just kiss you all night long.

Rondeau Redoublé Rendez-Vous

I just saw a vampire.
She tried to kiss me.
I think I just saw a vampire.
You don't have to be afraid just to please me.

And I don't wanna hear any
bullshit about 'I don't believe in vampires'
because I don't fucking believe
I just saw a vampire,

or believe in vampires, either.
She bit me like she's 13.
For god's sake, they're vampires.
She tried to kiss me.

Now, does everybody agree
we're dealing with vampires?
Melting on my tongue, summer slushies...
I think I just saw a vampire.

That's what vampires do, right?
Makes you wonder what could be
so bad it doesn't mind us thinking it's vampires.
You don't have to be afraid just to please me.

You disturb me.
Can we go and see the vampires?
You intrigue me.
I just saw a vampire.
I just met a vampire.

The Worst Is Yet to Come

He opens his bag, lays out his instruments with ritual care:
post-mortem knives, stakes, mallet, books, a poet's game.
A life that's just words words words shuffling my head.

Tear pages from the journal. Scatter them:
they float like mouths, every surface dusted with their powder.
Paper captured images of the wrong moments; time slips

around them without a ripple. This book fed what ate him up,
made it hungrier, so I have to read it like my food,
but all my food is poisoned. Father poisoned daughter

until even my breath was deadly, fresh flowers withering
in my grasp, my feet like erupted blueberries in batter.
Hair white, skin white, all colour drained long ago: scarlet

hands, scarlet stake, scarlet clouds; the colour of underwater
sea foam on a gray day; the colour of the moon as approached
in a spaceship; the colour of the beckoning brides of Dracula.

Moonlight streamed in a thick beam, dust particles gathering
brown moths, like a column of smoke. He wasn't dead while his
smell remained, mingling with the blue hyacinths in the kitchen.

The ᶜLittle Princess

I'm hungry, she said, like any child.
We were all hungry come the spring.
The girl would not eat with us. They
brought me her heart. I know it was hers.

Her blood-taste of chili and almonds,
of cardamom, of rosewater; the raw yolky
taste of dried apple teeth in my thumb.
Some say that I ate it. I did not:

I hung it with twine and robin-red rowan
berries and bulbs of garlic,
the way you'd crack a clock;
the way you'd crush a bone.

The goose-grease begins to melt,
glistens on my skin.

The Vampire Who Said He Was You

He bites. A mouth just bloodied.
The blood flood is the food of love.

A love gift utterly unasked for.
Death opened, like a black tree, blackly.

The box is only temporary, the
black bunched in there like a bat.

I bleed or sleep all the blackening morning,
separated from my house by headstones and corpses.

I am red meat, red hair; marble facades.
The corpse at the gate petrifies as I rise.

VAMANOS!

As far as God's concerned,
Menstrual blood is one rough-tough machine.
Peter Cushing does that all the time.
I want to walk the night and fall in love and drink.
Remember me. Dream of me.
Everyone else is just cocktails.

Shy

She was the most beautiful child I'd ever seen,
now she glowed with cold fire.

No sign of pallor or weakness, her voice
like plums warmed by sunlight.

She is mad. She is sensual.
Between her legs was the cane of a rose bush,

covered with reddish buds and brown thorns,
held tight between thighs stained with black filth.

I ripped it out. Blood ran in rivulets,
soaked the sheets.

She licked her heart, once, pushed it deep
into her chest, doll face seductive.

She stepped through the mirror,
took out scissors, cut her hair.

Her eyes were a woman's eyes; I could see it.
Colourless. Unreflecting. Unreflecting.

The Bride

The sheet covering her body, more beautiful and voluptuous
than ever, trembled. He knelt before her, straightening her
hair. Suddenly she was warm. Her legs opened. A hand fell out
below the sheet, jagged fingers twisting. Daylight's fading glow
flashed against her teeth, tingling laughter in the darkness.
The sheet slipped past her pale shoulders, her eyes glowing
hot. The fire smouldered, a red dawn. He placed a stake; he
struck. Fear left her face a blanket of white.

She's Going to Be Dazzling

My second reaction was horror:
I stared at the woman in the mirror
with terrifying sequin eyes.

Maybe the rest of me was in there,
in the shape of her red lips,
her ribs dusted with glitter.

I looked past the dizzying
beauty to see she drew lines
around herself, her lion's den,

and pushed me outside of them.
Her voice heavy, pulling me
down, swallowing me, hanging

in space.

I Want Some More

I could cry, but it's gross when I do.
Monsters, gutter royalty. Don't look away
from me. I am sick of defending my perilous
wounds with a chair. I might've had those
cardboard smiles, walked the road unrolled
like paper, long and smooth and magical,
but the sheet fell from my face and now
there's nowhere I can go. Black dirty things
that stink of toilet wall scrawls and smeared
basins. I haven't the tears for what you've
done to me. You understand nothing. The veil
is down. Burn in your mirror. Nurture grief
until it can love by itself – that's your child now.

Under the Eyes

They became troublesome:
the sound of sobbing
in a derelict bedroom,
where a cracked mirror
does not reflect.

Now all the village shun and
perpetuate the crimes
of subtle bitch schoolfriends,
manifesting imperceptible
revenant shadows.

Stones, Sticks

I see you. Someone did this, didn't they?
Every language is the language of murderers.

Are you sad? You need to strike back.
Split the skin open; expose the red flesh.

You've never done that, have you,
the laughing mouths of wounds?

Start now. Hit back. Hard.
Blood sprays with the force of a hose.

Then hit back harder. Use a weapon.
Make it rain in dark drops. Fall in pools.

You have a knife. It spills over skin
like light soaks up liquid.

Hit them more than you really dare
and then they'll stop.

Cut skin flutters like ribbons
in a little girl's hair.

You will be strong.

Thrall

I'm hungry. I can't eat sweets.
All that sugar, a white death.
You swore you would find me something to eat.

All those candy boys, those sugar girls,
pink and blue lines neatly ruled...
But you couldn't. We have nothing.

I will take that sweet. What is this taste,
clove of orient ash and papered sugar...
You swore you would find me something to eat.

I'm hungry. I can taste your morphine,
and your hash is dipped in the future.
We have nothing. We have nothing.

Interval

Marco pinned
and I felt the shape
in a little scalding pain
coiled on top of me,
writhing and biting.
I grew dazed and sick,
as if hammered at
by a tropical fever.
The lady tore Marco
to kill each other.

Lèche-vitrine

I sat and watched him writhe:
The tied-up boy, a sweet on the pillow,
eyes smouldering with banked fire –
He is the trouble I want to get in.

He'd charm girls with a flip of hair
until the earth crashed into the sun,
screams sweeter than cries of love.
He is used to girls screaming. He likes

to watch them snap, to be the drip
of water wearing on someone's soul.
Mouth soft, cheekbones sharp
as spilled ink, the pull of his teeth

staining his mouth along the swell
of his lower lip, ripe as nymphs,
eyebrows a mad black forest. I wasn't
careful as I licked his mouth.

I like when it hurts, the rush of warm
pouring out, ready to dive headfirst
into the meltdown I've been resisting,
a thin sound of shuddering violins.

Watch Her

I have bitten books that qualify me to be
vampiress of America. Who rivals?
Old books rot; that's a fact. Look at me.
I am eager, chafing, sure of my gift,
wanting only to train and teach.

I need fresh blood. No more hiding.
Aging giantesses, poetic godmothers...
gaudy scraps, shelves of finger marks
in dust. Time put their poison to sleep.
I turn books into bad dreams.

Soon, I'll eclipse my muse.
I'll break open my best eight, plunge
hyperdermic fangs of higher learning in
my gums for all the blood I swallowed.
Reader, unbury me with a word.

Solomonari

For Theo

The library is warm with golden tomes,
old leather and old folios, heavy pages,
a babble of conversation that smelled
of black cherries and clean cotton,
parting in violent rifts of drunken laughter,
books and maps, cracked spines,
razorblades between the pages.

Books aren't what you come to see.
This isn't exactly the safest place to hide,
walking on bones, skeletons ground to
gravel, no stone unpublished.

Pack your navy suitcases of aging paper
and cracked vellum; fill with schoolbooks
and too many pairs of clean socks.

Carry a map of scents in your head, a
whole world on a chunk of rock in the
middle of a bleak tile floor as if it were
dark water, clocks ticking disapprovingly
as candle-colours cut the newsprint dust.

There is a tradition the scholars protect.
The ghost of lights in your eyes
blow against the window.
Watch them explode against the glass.

Control

Me and my friend had this bet in eighth grade over who'd lose it first.

She was a disease you could catch, stuck in amber,
practically pregnant before I got my first kiss.

I must have imagined that glossy sheet of black hair
fitting her head like a helmet... strange little potbelly.

All virgins have rounded little bellies,
her skin a pink still burning from the bath.

Going to the bathroom in front of each other means
we have no secrets. We dream of boyfriends but only

feel comfortable with arms around another girl's waist.
A white pigeon flew by and saved her with a magic key,

she didn't become middle-heavy with leathery skin,
frosted hair, dirty clothes, stockings with runs.

I totally would be a slut if I could get away with it:
gilded waltzing cocks, wet plumage through my rooms.

I've never done any of that.
Now I have them. They just come out; I can't control them.

I'm a Monster

How do you know I'm a nice girl?
How can you say that?

This trick of my yesterdays is embarrassing.
Am I the girl who went to church every Sunday
and dressed up on Easter with hat and pocketbook
and matching patent leather shoes?

A scowl of sun struck down my mother.
A smoke that sears eyes took away my father.
I'd die if I wasn't already dead.
The days are false. The nights are true.

Vamping

I should have stayed in the tent with you,
but it's so uncivilized.

Last night I slept well, but frankly,
I kept hearing the words of that stupid song.

When I opened the dream, I was driving,
followed by a moon shadow.

I crashed into a looking-glass hotel with many men,
like I'd know where to find men in this bum-fucked town?

We had two hours before dawn.
I didn't know what to do with myself.

I keep hearing your words.
The needle got stuck on those words.

How I Am, Still

The telegram says you have gone away:
Proud, you halt the spiral stair;
you halt the clock.

You were condemned to serve the legal limit;
now you must play the straight man for a term.
You never altered your amused belief.

Solemn-eyed, about to vomit,
you thought of a means to end the vow,
a plot to halt the lethal flow.

The darkroom of your moonly mind
overcasts all others' noonday eye
to print your flaming birthspot image.

Queen-Sized

Three sheets from the rafters move softly,
lit only by early-morning sun. Shapes,
like tiny states on a map, spot the bluish-

ebony sheet, the kind that stains skin on hot nights.
In the height of summer the hundreds of rusty
marks give off only the faintest tang of iron.

But there is no smell on such a cold day as this.
It's about taking something hidden:
art and beauty and hard, glittering ideas

disposed of in secrecy, put on display.
Artsy chicks aren't allowed to shave their pits.
This is powerful. This is all me.

Squall

I like to drink my watercolour
swirled with a question mark.

Don't worry, earthquakes, the storm is coming:
ethereal elements, seasick walls of sound.
Don't worry, quakes. We heard them singing;
they'll replace your blood with bone-ground.

That is where they buried a saint,
and the singer danced on its grave.
Earthquakes, make your face less piquant,
fill the sky with firewaves.

There is no such thing as a single tear –
yours is companion to my own.
Deep brown fish of river, grainy gold of beer –
I need to stabilise the storm.

Assemble the girls. Bend the heavens.
Repopulate. Don't scowl. With the girls
transformed, that's a matter of opinion,
and I don't give a fuck about yours.

You and your words, obsessed

Day by day, colour by colour, touch by touch,
the discs of the brain revolve around his sifted
words, drifting to the dusty floor, cobwebs
mingling, keeping other pain at bay.

He made me feel special when I'd been invisible.
I retraced every line and stroke his pen made.
He certainly had a type: sensitive loners who read
poetry, who need someone to pour themselves into.

This lovers' prophecy turned in stubborn precision:
dour as grass, its words flat and virginal, carried on
wind. Nothing will happen that cannot be erased,
like glitter on the water between the scum and the sea.

Rosemary Remembers

Night is the hardest time to be alive.
I wake up here. Four am knows all my secrets.
Soon the sun will warm the stones under my feet.

I've waited half the night. Sometimes lovers rise,
sometimes they lie. Fingers cold as bone, as loneli-
ness, bones meeting and speaking in bone language.

Until I wake, my humanity is a dream depleted.
Something inside me remembers, will not forget.
What goes on between the dead is the dead's business.

Time ticks. The stone, the leaf, the unfound door,
the angel with its expression of soft stone idiocy,
a lily drooped, dead in stone. Dust.

Brood

I'm responsible for her welfare
I clothe her, shelter her, fed her
for seven years now every day
and night she earns her keep a
dozen times over the first few days
everything was white, white,
perfumes thick and dizzying,
flush with life, quite beautiful
but then she wilted I feed her
orgasm with eyes wide open, I
suppose what I had for her
wasn't enough She has a name
maybe, eventually, she'll die body
and spirit separate, like a huge bat
banging on the window

Self-worship and self-loathing

Don't ask me who I am. I am not ready for anything to happen.

The groundhog on the mountain did not run
toward midnight, but fatly scuttled into the splayed
fern, an inertia trap of certain green.

My senses seize the sick, soul-annihilating flux
of fear, the inner fear, the horny pot of sudden
terror that comes rolled in my blood, glory and
disgust I cannot keep still.

Biking home, talking to myself: There is no reason
for condemnation. Tonight mirrors the circumstances
of inner doubt, no sense of meaning, no stony feeling.
I am on the edge.

The morning sun is going up, a white mist to taunt me.
I haul the stone away from the tomb as the dream thumbs time.

Ruined

We wait until they turn her into an animal.
Who knows what she'll be like now with
the blood of so many people in her body.

Shame can't affect blood cells. So. All right.
Let's say you could take a skull,
break and chew it with sharp yellow teeth.

I meet plenty of guys who try to look tough
when they see carnage. And girls who push
me away, faces like hammers rising and falling.

A drop of dark black blood runs down
my hand between fingers and wrist, falls
onto the icy glass in a perfect circle.

Snow makes everything still.
What might she do, restored to full health?
Merge with the darkness and walk the night?

The Influence

Danger is a terrible addiction, but that's what I like:
the pleasure of picking the bad choice, my own path
to damnation, drowning in looping rapture,
boneless with relief.

There was a party and everyone died in a rain
of shimmering glass, fine as scattered sands,
driver slamming brakes, metal-scraped metal
wedged bone on road, occasional body parts
grinding into one another, blood a fizzy
strawberry soda of sherbet, copper and tears.

All the damage between us electrified the bodies
brushing against me, heads-bobbing bodies
lounging on car seats of velvet couches as lights
pulse and flash against a stained-glass windshield.

Heat spreading up my arm across my bare collar,
slivers of icy air chilling fingers, white kitten heels
sinking into red plush, the intoxicating dance of carnival,
the wildness of grief smeared over my skin in an explosion
like honey and milk and everything warm in the world,
words swallowed by the night.

I'm hungover, everyone's dead, and my root beer's gone.
One night you will ask for something I cannot give,
like a normal person who loved you.

Atmosphere

She's stealing my sleep from me
She moves through doors and windows
and minds and dreams, a shadow passing
the corridor in each pane of glass a dark
fingerprint glimpsed in the asphalt
and the world looks greenish and far away
through a tinted window,
an old shadow stolen during a lifetime,
How cruel to steal a shadow, how foolish
to measure a person's shadow, to fix it with a nail,
a painting with yellowing varnish
But I do believe in my own two fucking eyes,
and with my own two eyes I saw fucking:
She straddled him He came He spat in my face,
like mist, like a pitiful girl trying to disappear
in dark corners
I no longer dream about the girl in the light blue room,
but she won't leave my dream
I offered you the world, everyone in bed
breathing, dreaming, turning over.

Lost

I got ambushed in the bathroom. Cut my own image aging in the window, an eyeliner-glazed tinsel vision of sweat and melting mousse, hot leather and clove cigarettes, a brain of silver veils crackling with white noise.

No sweet disguises withstand the sun's stare.

How can you be so many girls to so many women, with our lion-red body and wings of glass?

I am young as ever: a girl who smells like jasmine and honey, someone who always sleeps on clean sheets, with storm-grey eyes, mink hair in a belljar bob curving a heartshaped face.

What is it I – a passionate, fragmentary girl – miss?

Polka-dot dress and proper-lady manners make me feel like I crawled out of a swamp. The spot I missed the last time I shaved will haunt me for eternity. My teeth encrusted, dirt under my fingernails.

Alone in my room. Between two worlds the Earth turns.

Baleful Posthumous Existence

Her voice is filled with sonorities, reverberations.
She herself is a cave of echoes.
Now you are at the place of annihilation.

The plucked heartstrings of a woman of metal!
Industrious spiders weave this rotten place.
She herself is a cave of echoes.

Sometimes the Countess will wake.
Sometimes the lark sings.
Industrious spiders weave this rotten place.

The white hands deal destiny.
Her beauty is a symptom of soulless.
Sometimes the lark sings.

The table is round where she lays out her Tarot.
Her fine China teeth picnic on corpses.
Her beauty is a symptom of soulless

spikes of spun sugar in Transylvanian forests.
Her voice is filled sonorities, reverberations.
Her fine China teeth picnic on corpses.
Now you are at the place of annihilation.

Acknowledgments

The author is indebted to the editors of the following publications, where some of these poems first appeared:
The *Emma Press Anthology of Contemporary Gothic Verse*, *Prototype Anthology 2*, *Dissections: the Journal of Contemporary Horror*, *Alice Says Go Fuck Yourself!*, *Tears in the Fence*, *Broken Spine*, *Three Drops from a Cauldron*, *Punk Noir*, the *Come as You Are* anthology, *Three Drops from a Cauldron Samhain 2016*, *Luna Luna*, *Five:2:One*, the *Autumn 2017 Singles Series* from Spooky Girlfriend Press, *Calamus*, *Yellow Chair Review*, *Printed Words*, *Glass: A Journal of Poetry*, *Voicemail Poems*, *Gingerbread House*, and *Rogue Agent*.

The author is also indebted to the following works from which these poems were sourced:
Poppy Z. Brite, *Lost Souls*; *Buffy the Vampire Slayer* (Mutant Enemy, 1997); Angela Carter, 'The Lady of the House of Love', in *The Bloody Chamber and Other Stories*; *From Dusk 'Til Dawn*, dir. by Robert Rodriguez (Miramax, 1996); *Doctor Who*: 'Vampires of Venice', dir. by Toby Whithouse (BBC Wales, 8 May 2010); Margie Fuston, *Vampires, Hearts & Other Dead Things*; Neil Gaiman, 'Snow, Glass, Apples' and 'Vampire Sestina', in *Angels & Visitations: A Miscellany*; Jim Hart, *Bram Stoker's Dracula* (ICM, Second draft screenplay, 16 April 1991); Joanne Harris, *The Evil Seed*; Sonia Hartl, *The Lost Girls: A Vampire Revenge Story*; Charlie Huston, *Already Dead*; Rachel Klein, *The Moth Diaries*; Elizabeth Kostova, *The Historian*; Jessica Lévai, *The Night Library of Sternendach: A Vampire Opera in Verse*; John Ajvide Lindqvist, *Let the Right One In*, trans. by Jack Thorne; Stephenie Meyer, *Breaking Dawn*; Sylvia Plath, *Collected Poems*, archive (Sylvia Plath Collection, Smith College); Anne Rice, *Interview with the Vampire*; Anne Rice and Neil Jordan, *Interview with the Vampire* (ICM, second draft screenplay adaptation, 1993); Chris Riddell, *Goth Girl and the Fête Worse than Death*; Caleb Roehrig, *The Fell of Dark*; Bram Stoker, *Dracula*; *True Blood*, dir. by Alan Ball (HBO, 2008); David Wellington, *13 Bullets: A Vampire Tale*.

Lay out your undead

Ingram Content Group UK Ltd.
Milton Keynes UK
UKHW040117060523
421313UK00006B/484

9 781915 760104